The Unofficial Guide to Hamilton
Everything You Need to Know about the
Hit Broadway Musical!
Authored by Sarah P. Patrick

Copyright © 2016 Sarah P. Patrick

ISBN-13: 978-1530899388
ISBN-10: 1530899389

Printed in the United States of America

THE UNOFFICIAL GUIDE TO

HAMILTON

Everything You Need to Know

About the Hit Broadway Musical!

SARAH P. PATRICK

THE UNOFFICIAL GUIDE TO HAMILTON

Section 1: The Musical

Section 2: Planning Your Trip to See Hamilton

Section 3: Additional Information

Section One

THE MUSICAL

Chapter One

INTRODUCTION

*T*he hit musical *Hamilton* has taken Broadway by storm! By every measure of success, it is a huge blockbuster, and the momentum does not appear to be slowing any time soon!

From a box office perspective, *Hamilton* is sold out on Broadway for the foreseeable future. The Original Cast Recording Album is a best-seller and Grammy winner! A Chicago version of the musical is set to open an extended run starting in the fall of 2016. Fans line the street to catch a glimpse of the cast, and the stage door appearances after the show are the stuff of legends.

The court of public opinion has ruled and *Hamilton* is a hit! Critics rave about the show. Fans adore the music, the cast, the staging, and the message of

Hamilton! If you are one of these fans, this book is for you! It will give you valuable information about every aspect of the show and essential strategies to make seeing *Hamilton* LIVE the very best experience possible. I will even include some top-secret tips about increasing your chances of winning the lottery, getting autographs and photos of the stars, and even where the cast and crew hang out around town!

I am in no way affiliated with the official production of the musical ... so these tips and tricks come to you unfiltered and unbiased. My best piece of advice comes first: If you have not seen the show, go see it! It will exceed every expectation and be worth every dollar you spend!

And now ... on with the show!

Sarah Patrick

Chapter Two

HISTORY

The story of this musical begins with a biography about Alexander Hamilton, researched and written by Ron Chernow. This book was published in 2005 but was not read by Lin-Manuel Miranda until a few years later. Miranda read the biography while on vacation, and he immediately pictured a hip-hop immigrant story.

At the time, Lin-Manuel Miranda had another hit musical on his hands, *In the Heights*. During his spare time, he worked on the music and songs for the Hamilton project, which was originally called "The Hamilton Mixtape." The first song on The Hamilton Mixtape, "Alexander Hamilton," would evolve into the opening number of the musical. The song "My Shot" followed, but took nearly a year to write as Miranda worked to capture the brilliance of Hamilton's turn of phrase.

The work was performed as a workshop production in 2013, with original cast members Lin-Manuel Miranda, Daveed Diggs, and Chris Jackson in their current roles.

The musical in its current form opened Off Broadway at The Public Theater in February, 2015. The show opened on Broadway at the Richard Rodgers Theatre in August, 2015.

Chapter Three

ALEXANDER HAMILTON

*I*n this chapter, you'll find the key events from Alexander Hamilton's life that will help you understand both the man and the musical:

Alexander Hamilton was born on January 11th in either 1755 or 1757 in the West Indies.

Hamilton was born out of wedlock to Rachel Faucette, a married woman of British and French Huguenot descent, and James A. Hamilton.

Alexander Hamilton's mother died in 1768, leaving him orphaned. Hamilton later became a clerk at a trading charter. He was an avid reader and writer.

In 1772, Hamilton wrote an account of a hurricane that hit their island for a local newspaper. The essay impressed many people, and a fund was collected to send Alexander to North America to further his education.

Hamilton attended King's College in New York City, which is now called Columbia University. He met Aaron Burr shortly after arriving in the colonies, and their paths would cross multiple times over the next three decades.

In 1774, Samuel Seabury, a local farmer, published a series of pamphlets supporting loyalty to England. Hamilton wrote a number of strong responses against this, including one titled "The Farmer Refuted."

In 1775, at the start of the Revolutionary War, Hamilton joined a militia company. He famously stole British cannons while under fire in New York City. In the next year, he rose to captain of a provincial artillery company.

He was noticed by General George Washington and hired to be Washington's senior aide. During the war, Hamilton became close friends with several fellow officers, including Marquis de Lafayette and John Laurens.

During the war, Hamilton was George Washington's "right-hand man" and wrote much of his correspondence. He went on important missions to communicate to generals and offered counsel and advice in all areas. Hamilton wanted to be a leader in combat, but he was too valuable to Washington as an aide.

In 1779, Hamilton met the Schuyler sisters: Angelica, Eliza, and Peggy. He would marry Eliza but remained very close to Angelica throughout his life.

In February of 1781, Hamilton resigned from his position as aide to General Washington. In July of 1781, Hamilton was given the combat leadership position he desired. In the Battle of Yorktown, Hamilton led three battalions. With the help of the French, these forces defeated the British, and the war was over.

In 1782, Alexander and his wife, Eliza, had their first child, Philip, who was killed by George Eacker in a duel at the age of 19. Alexander and his wife had seven other children.

After the war, Hamilton was elected to the Congress of the Confederation, practiced law, and founded the Bank of New York.

Hamilton was instrumental in the Constitutional Convention and wrote many of The Federalist Papers, which defended and explained the Constitution.

Hamilton became the Secretary of the Treasury under the first president, George Washington. He argued that the federal government needed to be strong and argued that the federal government fund a national debt, assume state's debts, and create a national bank. This would be funded by a tariff on imports and a tax on whiskey.

Thomas Jefferson and James Madison opposed these ideas and formed a coalition to oppose them, which would later become the Democratic Republican Party. Hamilton also put together a network of people on his side, which would become the Federalist Party.

In 1791, Hamilton worked to get his proposed ideas through Congress. To overcome opposition, he struck a compromise with Jefferson and Madison where the U.S. Capitol would be moved south to Washington, D.C. In exchange for this, Madison rounded up the votes to get Hamilton's ideas through Congress.

During this time in 1791, Hamilton had an affair with Maria Reynolds. He would later be blackmailed by Reynold's husband, and eight years later, this scandal became public and stopped Hamilton from seeking the presidency.

In 1794, Hamilton supported the Jay Treaty to improve relations with Britain. Jefferson opposed this and preferred to support France, where he had spent his time during the Revolutionary War.

In 1795, Hamilton returned to New York to practice law. In the election of 1800, Thomas Jefferson and Aaron Burr tied for the presidency in the Electoral College. Hamilton supported Jefferson, which tipped the election in his favor. Hamilton disagreed with most of what Jefferson stood for but appreciated the fact that he had strong beliefs.

Aaron Burr returned to New York and ran for Governor in 1804. Hamilton campaigned against Burr.

Aaron Burr challenged Alexander to a duel in 1804. During the duel, Burr shot Hamilton, who died the next day, July 12, 1804.

Alexander's wife would live another 50 years, during which time she worked tirelessly with her sister, Angelica, to organize Hamilton's papers and preserve his legacy.

Chapter Four

TEN THINGS YOU NEED TO KNOW ... ABOUT HAMILTON!

1. Martha Washington named one of her tomcats after Hamilton.

2. There are three duels in the musical:

   Charles Lee vs. John Laurens
   George Eacker vs. Philip Hamilton
   Aaron Burr vs. Alexander Hamilton

3. Eliza Hamilton outlived her husband by 50 years. She founded the first public orphanage in New York.

4. Eliza Hamilton helped Dolly Madison raise the funds for the Washington Monument.

5. Alexander Hamilton was the founder of the nation's financial system.

6. Alexander Hamilton was the founder of the Federalist Party.

7. Alexander Hamilton is considered the Father of the United States Coast Guard.

8. Alexander Hamilton was the founder of *The New York Post*.

9. Alexander Hamilton was the first Secretary of the Treasury.

10. Hamilton was buried in the Trinity Churchyard Cemetery in Manhattan. Eliza and Angelica are buried there, as well.

Chapter Five

HAMILTON ON BROADWAY AND BEYOND

The story of the musical *Hamilton* opened off-Broadway at The Public Theater in February of 2015.

Hamilton premiered on Broadway at the Richard Rodgers Theatre on July 13, 2015. This is the same theater that was home to Lin-Manuel Miranda's musical, *In the Heights*.

Hamilton will have a separate non-touring production at the PrivateBank Theatre in Chicago starting September 27, 2016.

The first national tour of *Hamilton* is scheduled to begin at San Francisco's SHN Orpheum Theatre in March 2017, where it is scheduled to run for 21 weeks. The production will then move to the Hollywood Pantages Theatre in Los Angeles.

Section Two

PLANNING YOUR TRIP TO SEE HAMILTON

Chapter Six

GETTING TICKETS

The most difficult part of any trip to see *Hamilton* on Broadway will be getting your tickets. The show is sold out through the foreseeable future, and when new tickets become available, they are gone in minutes.

This does not mean it is impossible to see the show … I saw the show just last week, and it was amazing! Acquiring tickets does require some advanced planning and strategizing … so here is a rundown of you best options:

Purchasing Direct

The safest and most secure way to purchase tickets to the show is through the official *Hamilton* website or box office. Unfortunately, this also may mean it will be a year or more before you actually attend the show.

To increase your odds of getting tickets, consider buying single tickets, instead of a group of seats together. You will not be talking to your friends during the show—it's that good ... and you will have a lifetime to talk about it after it's over!

The official website where you can purchase tickets is: www.Hamiltonbroadway.com.

Single tickets are occasionally available ... obviously, weekday show tickets are more likely to become available than tickets for shows on the weekends.

INSIDER TIP!

Don't worry too much about your seat location. There is not a bad seat in the house. Every location has its advantages: Sit closer and you will be able to see facial expressions. Sit farther back and you will marvel at the amazing rotating stage and innovative lighting. You can hear every word of every song from any seat ... so if you can get a ticket, grab it and go!

Resale Sites

There are a number of resale sites that allow you to purchase tickets to the show from other people. My advice is to stick to a nationally-known reputable site such as Stub-Hub. They offer a guarantee that your tickets are valid and real. A quick check of this site shows that there are dozens of tickets available for almost every future date ... but you will pay much more than face value for the tickets. The last time I attended the show I purchased a seat in the balcony. The face value of the ticket was $50, but I paid $300 for the ticket. The show is a bargain at any price ... so save your pennies and pick a date!

INSIDER TIP!

If you purchase your ticket from a website such as Stub-Hub, be sure to print your ticket at home prior to coming to the theater. The theater box office does not have a printer you can use to print your tickets, and you will not be allowed in without a ticket!

The Lottery

This option is a longshot … but always worth a try. There is an online lottery for about 25 tickets to each show. You can sign up online the day of the show to win one or two tickets. If you win the tickets, they are very inexpensive and very good seats! You will be notified that you won a few hours before the show and will only have 60 minutes to pay for the tickets online. You then show up an hour before the show to pick up your tickets, and you are in! No one will say how many people sign up for the lottery each day, but my guess is thousands … based on how many times I have lost!

Full details about the daily lottery for show tickets can be found at the official website here: www.Hamiltonbroadway.com.

INSIDER TIP!

Make sure everyone in your party signs up for the lottery. The more people you enter, the better chance you have of winning! Each person can enter once, and you must show a photo ID with a matching name to pick up the tickets.

Chapter Seven

GETTING TO NEW YORK

*N*ow that you have your tickets for the show, it is time to start planning your trip! The first step of that process is to get to New York City!

The best way to get to New York depends on where you live. If flying is your best option, there are three airports to choose from: John F. Kennedy International Airport, LaGuardia Airport, and Newark International Airport.

Each of these airports is served by a variety of major airlines, and each is less than an hour cab ride from the show (not including traffic delays, which vary based on the time of day!).

INSIDER TIP!

Many people forget to look at the Newark, New Jersey airport, but I have had great luck finding airfare to this airport; and as long as you don't arrive during the morning or afternoon rush hour, it is only about 45 minutes from the theater!

Chapter Eight

WHERE TO STAY

New York City has hundreds of hotels in a variety of price ranges. Many of these hotels are located right in the Theater District, which is where you want to be. This chapter includes a listing of the closest hotels to the theater, along with my top recommendation.

The very best hotel to stay in if you are seeing the show is the Marriott Marquis Times Square. This hotel is located right on Times Square in New York City, but, more important, it is located right next to the Richard Rodgers Theatre, home to *Hamilton*!

You will walk 10 steps out the door of this hotel and be at the door of the theater. The last time we were at the show, two cast members walked right through the first floor atrium of this hotel on their way to lunch and back to the theater. If you want to be in the heart of the action, this is the place to stay.

The best part about staying at this hotel is that you can run back and forth to your room. You may wish to see the cast members arrive early in the day, then go to your room to change clothes, then see the show, then stop by your room to grab a jacket, and then see the cast at the stage door. This is only possible if you are staying close by, and no hotel is as close as the Marriott Marquis Times Square.

Other hotels within walking distance of the theater include:

The Westin New York at Times Square
270 W 43rd Street
New York, NY
(212) 201-2700

Renaissance New York Times Square Hotel
714 Seventh Avenue
New York, NY
(212) 261-5100

Crowne Plaza Times Square Manhattan
1605 Broadway
New York, NY
(212) 977-4000

Paramount Hotel
235 W 46th Street
New York, NY
(212) 764-5500

Sanctuary Hotel
132 W 47th Street
New York, NY
(800) 388-8988

DoubleTree Suites by Hilton Times Square
1568 Broadway
New York, NY
1-800-222-TREE

Mayfair Hotel
242 W 49th Street
New York, NY
(212) 586-0300

The Michelangelo Hotel
152 W 51st Street
New York, NY
(212) 765-1900

Amsterdam Court Hotel
226 W 50th Street
New York, NY
(212) 459-1000

Novotel
226 W 52nd Street
New York, NY
(800) 515-5679

Econo Lodge
767 Eighth Avenue
New York, NY
(212) 246-1991

Hampton Inn Manhattan Times Square Central
220 W 41 Street
New York, NY
(212) 221-1188

Hyatt Times Square
135 West 45th Street
New York, NY
(646) 364-1234

Room Mate Grace Hotel
125 W 45th Street
New York, NY
(212) 354-2323

Intercontinental New York Times Square
300 W 44th Street
New York, NY
(212) 803-4500

Hilton Garden Inn Times Square Central
136 West 42nd Street
New York, NY
1-877-STAY-HGI

Hotel 41
206 W 41st Street
New York, NY
212-703-8600

RIU Hotel
733 Eighth Avenue
New York, NY
(646) 864-1100

The Manhattan at Times Square Hotel
790 Seventh Avenue
New York, NY
(212) 581-3300

The French Quarters Guest Apartments
346 W 46th Street
New York, NY
(212) 359-6652

Hotel St. James
109 W 45th Street
New York, NY
(212) 221-3600

The Muse Hotel
130 W 46th Street
New York, NY
(212) 485-2400

Night Hotel Times Square on 47th Street
157 West 47th Street
New York, NY
1-866-950-7829

Sheraton New York Times Square Hotel
811 Seventh Avenue
New York, NY
(212) 581-1000

Casablanca Hotel
147 W 43rd Street
New York, NY
(212) 869-1212

Comfort Inn Times Square
129 W 46th Street
New York, NY
(212) 221-2600

The Pearl
233 W 49th Street
New York, NY
(800) 801-3457

The Chatwal, a Luxury Collection Hotel, New York
130 W 44th Street
New York, NY
888.5.CHATWAL

Hilton Garden Inn Times Square
790 Eighth Avenue
New York, NY
1-877-STAY-HGI

Hampton Inn Manhattan Times Square North
851 Eighth Avenue
New York, NY
1-800-HAMPTON

Broadway at Times Square Hotel
129 W 46th Street
New York, NY
(212) 221-2600

Hotel Mela
120 W 44th Street
New York, NY
(212) 710-7000

The Knickerbocker
6 Times Square
New York, NY
(212) 204-4980

Hilton Times Square
234 West 42nd Street
New York, NY
1-800-HILTONS

citizenM Hotel
218 W 50th Street
New York, NY
212-461-3638

TRYP by Wyndham
234 W 48th Street
New York, NY
(212) 246-8800

New York Inn
765 8th Avenue
New York, NY
(212) 247-5400

Row NYC
700 Eighth Avenue
New York, NY
(888) 352-3650

The Time Hotel
224 W 49th Street
New York, NY
(877) 846-3692

W New York - Times Square
1567 Broadway
New York, NY
(212) 930-7400

Millennium Broadway Hotel New York
145 West 44th Street
New York, NY
(212) 768-4400

Chapter Nine

WHERE TO EAT

*I*f you are going to experience all that New York City has to offer, you need to eat! The Richard Rodgers Theatre is located in the heart of New York's Theater District and is, therefore, surrounded by great restaurants to eat at before and after the show. This chapter includes a complete listing of nearby restaurants, including five of my highest recommendations!

Top Recommendation: Patzeria

Patzeria is an authentic New York pizzeria located right across the street from the theater! You can order a slice of pizza and watch the front door and stage door of the theater right from the sidewalk! We know the cast and crew go to Patzeria on occasion. There is even a poster inside the restaurant signed by the full cast. Cast members will also occasionally tweet about their favorite slice at this restaurant ... I recommend the "Grandma's Slice"... and so does George Washington!

Other Recommendations:

Juniors
1515 Broadway # 1
New York, NY

Juniors is a landmark restaurant in the Theater District and a great place to grab a bite to eat before or after the show! The best part: you have a good chance of running into a cast member or two here; we know they often show up to the theater with coffee from Juniors! Located just through the atrium of the Marriott Marquis Times Square Hotel, this restaurant is one block from the Richard Rogers Theatre! Not fancy, just good food and a good chance to see a cast member!

City Kitchen
700 8th Avenue at 44th Street
New York, NY 10036

Tourists will often walk right past this restaurant because it is located above street level on the corner of 44th Street and 8th Avenue. (If you are standing at Shake Shack and look up diagonally across the intersection, you can see right into the restaurant.) This restaurant is a food-court style cafeteria with multiple options. It's loaded with locals, and cast members definitely eat here on occasion!

Sardi's
234 West 44th Street
New York, NY
Between Broadway and 8th Ave

Sardis has been a staple of the Theater District for years and is known as a go-to place for cast and crew members from many musicals and plays in the areas. The restaurant even has a special discount for cast and crew members on Wednesdays between the matinee show and the evening show. This makes Sardis a great place to people watch ... you never know who you will see!

Joe Allen's Pub
326 W 46th Street
New York, NY

Another landmark of the Theater District, Joe Allen's Pub offers great food at reasonable prices. The last time I attended *Hamilton*, I ate dinner here before the show. The very next day, Lin-Manuel Miranda tweeted a picture of himself eating at the restaurant! Sometimes you get lucky, and sometimes you just miss!

Restaurant Row

Located just down the road from the Richard Rodgers Theatre is "Restaurant Row." This is a collection of over 20 restaurants that cater to the pre-theater crowd. You will find every cuisine and type of food within this two-block area on 46th Street, a short walk from *Hamilton*!

Here is a list of restaurants on "Restaurant Row:"

Barbetta Restaurant
321 W 46th Street
New York, NY 10036
Phone: (212) 246-9171

Bangkok House
360 W 46th Street
New York, NY 10036
Phone: (212) 541-5943

Becco
355 W 46th Street
New York, NY 10036
Phone: (212) 397-7597

Bistecca Fiorentina
317 W 46th Street
New York, NY 10036
Phone: (212) 258-3232

Brasserie Athenee
300 W 46th Street
New York, NY 10036
Phone: (212) 399-1100

Brazil Brazil
328 W 46th Street
New York, NY 10036
Phone: (212) 957-4300

Bourbon Street Bar & Grille
346 W 46th Street
New York, NY 10036
Phone: (212) 245-2030

Da Rosina Ristorante Italiano
342 W 46th Street
New York, NY 10036
Phone: (212) 977-7373

Don't Tell Mama
343 W 46th Street
New York, NY 10036
Phone: (212) 757-0788

Hourglass Tavern
373 W 46th Street
New York, NY 10036
Phone: (212) 265-2060

La Pulperia
371 W 46 Street
Between 8th and 9th Avenues
New York, NY 10036
Phone: (212) 956-3055

La Rivista Ristorante
313 W 46th Street
New York, NY 10036
Phone: (212) 245-1707

Lattanzi Restaurant
359 W 46th Street
New York, NY 10036
Phone: (212) 315-0980

Le Rivage
340 W 46th Street
New York, NY 10036
Phone: (212) 765-7374

Meson Sevilla Ristorante
344 W 46th Street
New York, NY 10036
Phone: (212) 262-5890

Orso
322 W 46th Street
New York, NY 10036
Phone: (212) 489-7212

Ritz Bar & Lounge
369 W 46th Street
New York, NY 10036
Phone: (212) 977-3884

Sangria 46
338 W 46th Street
New York, NY 10036
Phone: (212) 581-8482

Sushi of Gari
347 W 46th Street
New York, NY 10036
Phone: (212) 957-0046

Here is a listing of other restaurants near the Theater District:

48 Lounge
1221 Ave of the Americas
New York, NY
American Traditional / Cocktail Lounge

Angus' Cafe Bistro
258 West 44th Street
New York, NY
Steakhouse

Applebee's
205 W 50th Street
Between 7th Ave and Broadway
American Traditional

Applebee's
234 West 42nd Street
New York, NY
Between 7th Ave & 8th Ave
American Traditional

Aureole
135 West 42nd Street
New York, NY
Progressive American

B.B. King Blues Club and Grill
237 West 42nd Street
New York, NY
American Traditional

Bar Americain
152 W 52nd Street
New York, NY
American

Bella Vita Brick Oven Pizza
211 West 43rd Street
New York, NY
Between 7th Ave and 8th Ave
Pizzeria

Blue Fin
1567 Broadway
New York, NY
Seafood

Bobby Van's
120 West 45th Street
New York, NY
Steakhouse

Bombay Masala
148 West 49th Street
New York, NY
Between 6th Ave and 7th Ave
Indian

Bond 45
221 West 46th Street
New York, NY
Between 6th and 7th Aves.
Italian Steakhouse

Bourbon Street
346 West 46th Street
New York, NY
Restaurant Row, Between 8th Ave and 9th Ave
American Traditional / Cajun

Brasserie 1605
1605 Broadway
New York, NY
Between 48th St and 49th St (Crowne Plaza Times
Square)
French

Brazil Grill
787 8th Avenue
New York, NY
At 48th Street
Brazilian

Broadway Thai at Tom and Toon
241 West 51st Street
New York, NY
Thai-American Fusion

Brooklyn Diner
155 West 43rd Street
New York, NY
Diner

Bubba Gump Shrimp Co.
1501 Broadway
New York, NY
At 44th St
American Traditional / Seafood / Southern

Buca di Beppo
1540 Broadway
New York, NY
Italian

BXL Cafe
125 West 43rd Street
New York, NY
Belgian

Ca Va
310 West 44th Street
New York, NY
Between 8th Ave and 9th Ave (InterContinental New
York Times Square)
French

Cafe Cranberry
115 W 45th Street
New York, NY
American Traditional

Cafe Un Deux Trois
123 West 44th Street
New York, NY
Between 6th Ave and Broadway
French

Carmine's
200 West 44th Street
New York, NY
Italian

Carve: Unique Sandwiches & Pizza
760 8th Avenue
New York, NY
American

Casa Nonna
310 West 38th Street
New York, NY
Between 8th and 9th Avenues
Italian

Ceci
46 West 46th Street
New York, NY
Between 5th and 6th Avenues
Italian

Characters Grill
243 West 54th Street
New York, NY
American Traditional

Charlie Palmer at the Knick
6 Times Square
New York, NY
Progressive American

Chevys
259 West 42nd Street
New York, NY
Mexican

Churrascaria Plataforma
316 West 49th Street
New York, NY
Between 8th and 9th Avenues
Brazilian

Cielo at the Mayfair
242 West 49th Street
New York, NY
Italian

Cock & Bull
23 West 45th Street
New York, NY
Between 5th and 6th Avenues
British Pub

Connolly's
121 West 45th Street
New York, NY
Between 6th Ave and 7th Ave
American Traditional / Irish Pub

Cosmic Diner
888 8th Avenue
New York, NY
Diner

Da Marino
220 West 49th Street
New York, NY
Italian

Da Tommaso
903 8th Avenue
New York, NY
Italian

Dallas BBQ
241 W 42nd Street
New York, NY
Barbecue

db Bistro Moderne
55 West 44th Street
New York, NY
Between 5th and 6th Avenues
Modern French-American

Dervish
146 West 47th Street
New York, NY
Between 6th Ave and 7th Ave
Turkish

Dos Caminos Mexican Restaurant
1567 Broadway
New York, NY
Between Broadway and 7th Avenue
Mexican

E&E Grill House
233 West 49th Street
New York, NY
Steakhouse

Ellen's Stardust Diner
1650 Broadway
New York, NY
Diner

Emmett O'Lunney's
210 West 50th Street
New York, NY
At Broadway
American Traditional / Irish Pub

Five Napkin Burger
630 9th Avenue
New York, NY
American Traditional

Frankie and Johnnie's Steakhouse
320 West 46th Street
New York, NY
Steakhouse

Gallagher's Steak House
228 West 52nd Street
New York, NY
Steakhouse

Glass House Tavern
252 W. 47th Street
New York, NY
American Traditional

Gossip Bar & Restaurant
733 9th Avenue
New York, NY
Between 49th and 50th Street
American

Guy's American Kitchen & Bar
220 West 44th Street
New York, NY
Between 7th and 8th Avenues
American

Hard Rock Cafe
1501 Broadway
New York, NY
Between 44th St and 43rd St
American Traditional

Haru
229 W 43rd Street, Unit 221
New York, NY
Japanese

Havana Central
151 West 46th Street
New York, NY
Between 6th Ave and 7th Ave
Cuban

Heartland Brewery and Chophouse
127 West 43rd Street
New York, NY
Steakhouse

Hurley's Saloon
232 West 48th Street
New York, NY
Between Broadway and 8th Ave
American Traditional / Irish Pub

Iguana
240 West 54th Street
New York, NY
Mexican

Iron Bar Restaurant & Lounge
713 8th Ave
New York, NY
American Traditional

John's Pizzeria
260 West 44th Street
New York, NY
Pizzeria

Kodama Sushi
301 West 45th Street
New York, NY
Japanese

L'ybane Restaurant
709 8th Avenue
New York, NY
French

La Masseria
235 W 48th Street # 2
New York, NY
Italian

Langan's Pub & Restaurant
150 W 47th Street
New York, NY
American Traditional

Latitude Bar & Grill
783 8th Avenue
New York, NY
American Traditional

Lindy's
825 7th Avenue
New York, NY
American Traditional

Luna Piena
224 West 51st Street
New York, NY
Between Broadway and 8th Ave
Italian

Maison Kayser
1800 Broadway
New York, NY
French

Maria's Mont Blanc
315 West 48th Street
New York, NY
Between 8th Ave and 9th Ave
European

Matt's Grill
932 Eighth Avenue
New York, NY
Between 55th St and 56th St
American Traditional

Mi Nidito
852 8th Ave # 1
New York, NY
Mexican

Mr. Robata
1674 Broadway
New York, NY
Japanese

Nanking
1634 Broadway # 2
New York, NY
Chinese

Natsumi
226 West 50th Street
New York, NY
Between Broadway and 8th Ave
Japanese

Num Pang
148 W 48th Street
New York, NY
American

O'Lunney's Pub
145 West 45th Street
New York, NY
Between 6th Ave and Broadway
American Traditional / Irish Pub

Olive Garden
2 Times Square
New York, NY
At 47th St
Italian

Palm Restaurant Westside
250 West 50th Street
New York, NY
At 8th Ave
Steakhouse

Paramount Bar & Grill
325 W 46th Street
New York, NY
American Traditional

Pasta Lover's Trattoria
142 W 49th Street
New York, NY
Italian

Paul's on Times Square
136 W 42nd Street
New York, NY
Italian

Peking Duck House
236 East 53rd Street
New York, NY
Chinese

Pergola Des Artistes
252 West 46th Street
New York, NY
Between Broadway and 8th Ave
French

Pigalle
790 8th Avenue # 2
New York, NY
French

Planet Hollywood
1540 Broadway
New York, NY
At 45th Street
American Traditional

Playwright Celtic Pub
732 8th Avenue
New York, NY
Between 45th St and 46th St
American Traditional / Irish Pub

Playwright Tavern
202 West 49th Street
New York, NY
Between Broadway and 7th Ave
American Traditional / Irish Pub

Pongsri Restaurant
244 West 48th Street
New York, NY
Thai

Quinn's NYC
356 W. 44th Street
New York, NY
Between 8th and 9th Avenues
Irish Pub

R Lounge
714 7th Avenue
New York, NY
Between 47th St and 48th St, Renaissance Times
Square Hotel
American Traditional / Cocktail Lounge

Red Lobster
5 Times Square
New York, NY
At 41st St
Seafood

Rosie O'Grady's
149 West 46th Street
New York, NY
Between 6th Ave and Broadway
Seafood / Steakhouse

Ruby Tuesday
7 Times Square
New York, NY
American Traditional

Russian Samovar
256 West 52nd Street
New York, NY
Russian

Russian Vodka Room
265 West 52nd Street
New York, NY
Russian

Saju
120 West 44th Street
New York, NY
Between 6th Ave and Broadway
French

Scarlatto
250 West 47th Street
New York, NY
Italian

Schnipper's
620 8th Avenue
New York, NY
at 41st Street
American Traditional

Serafina
224 West 49th Street
New York, NY
Italian

Shake Shack
691 8th Ave
New York, NY
American

Shula's American Steakhouse
270 West 43rd Street
New York, NY
At 8th Avenue
Steakhouse

Smith's Bar and Restaurant
701 8th Avenue
New York, NY
American Traditional / Irish Pub

Social Bar and Grill
795 8th Avenue
New York, NY
American Traditional / Irish Pub

Sofia's Ristorante
221 W 46th Street # 1
New York, NY
Italian

Sombrero
303 West 48th Street
At 8th Avenue
New York, NY
Mexican

Sosa Borella
832 8th Avenue
New York, NY
Argentine / Italian

Southern Hospitality
645 9th Avenue
New York, NY
Corner of 45th Street and 9th Avenue
American / Barbecue

T.G.I. Friday's
1552 Broadway
New York, NY
American Traditional

T.G.I. Friday's
761 7th Avenue
New York, NY
At 50th Street
American Traditional

Ted's Montana Grill
110 West 51st Street
New York, NY
West 51st Street at 6th Avenue
American / American Traditional

Tender
130 W 47th Street
New York, NY
Steakhouse

Thalia
828 8th Avenue
New York, NY
Progressive American

The House of Brews
363 West 46th Street
New York, NY
Restaurant Row, Between 8th Ave and 9th Ave
American Traditional / Irish Pub

The Irish Pub
837 7th Avenue
New York, NY
American Traditional / Irish Pub

The Lambs Club
132 West 44th Street
New York, NY
Between 6th Avenue and Broadway on 44th Street
American

The Long Room
120 W 44th Street
New York, NY
American Traditional

The Mean Fiddler
266 West 47th Street
New York, NY
American Traditional / Irish Pub

Toloache
251 West 50th Street
New York, NY
Mexican

Tonic Times Square
727 7th Avenue
New York, NY
Between 48th St and 49th St
American Traditional

Tony's DiNapoli
147 West 43rd Street
New York, NY
Between 6th Ave and 7th Ave
Italian

Trattoria Trecolori
254 West 47th Street
New York, NY
Between Broadway and 8th Ave
Italian

TSQ Brasserie
723 7th Avenue
New York, NY
American Traditional

Urbo
11 Times Square
New York, NY
At 8th Avenue
Eclectic

Utsav
1185 Avenue of the Americas
New York, NY
Between 6th and 7th Avenues
Indian

Victor's Cafe 52
236 West 52nd Street # 1
New York, NY
Caribbean

Virgil's Real BBQ
152 West 44th Street
New York, NY
Between Broadway and 6th Ave
Barbecue

West End Bar & Grill
813 8th Avenue
New York, NY
Progressive American

Chapter Nine.5

SECRET CHAPTER
FOR INSIDERS ONLY!

$\mathcal{W}$ell, if you have made it this far in the book, you are ready for my top-secret, insider-only chapter!

The cast of *Hamilton* loves to go bowling! They will often go bowling as a group after the show. Sometimes they will team up and bowl against the cast of another nearby musical! Pay attention to their Twitter feeds as they often tweet while they are bowling!

Because of this information, here is a listing of the three bowling alleys near the Richard Rodgers Theatre:

Frames Bowling Lounge
550 9th Avenue
New York, NY 10018
framesnyc.com
(212) 268-6909

Bowlmor Times Square
222 W 44th Street
New York, NY 10036
bowlmor.com
(212) 680-0012

Lucky Strike Manhattan
624-660 W. 42nd Street
New York, NY 10036
bowlluckystrike.com
(646) 829-0170

Chapter Ten

MAKING THE MOST OF YOUR EXPERIENCE

*A*ttending *Hamilton* should be an event! You work so hard to get tickets and get to the show, so rather than just arriving at show time and leaving once it is over, you can get so much more out of your experience if you plan ahead and extend your day!

Early in the Day

Arrive to the Theater District early to see all that Times Square has to offer! See the ball that falls on New Year's Eve and shop at the very best stores!

Cast Arrival

The cast will usually arrive at the theater a little more than three hours before the show. I like to grab a slice of pizza at Patzeria and wait on the sidewalk to watch them arrive. The stage door is labeled clearly, and most cast members will enter through it. The stage door is much less crowded before the show than it is after the show, so this is a great time to get autographs and photos.

Showtime

I like to enter the theater as soon as the doors open so I can experience both the beauty of the theater and the set design. Don't be intimidated by the long lines to get in—the line moves quickly, and you will soon be in your seat. This is a great time to buy your official *Hamilton* gear, as well … don't leave the theater without it!

Stage Door

After the show, head immediately to the stage door. It won't be hard to find, there will be hundreds or thousands of people there. Get as close to the barricade as possible to give yourself the best chance of getting an autograph or a photo.

Chapter Eleven

THE STAGE DOOR EXPERIENCE

There is nothing on Broadway that compares to the *Hamilton* Stage Door experience! It is complete chaos, and you're almost guaranteed a chance to see some of the cast members up close if you are willing to battle the crowds and wait your turn.

The stage door is located just down the street from the main entrance to the theater. It is clearly labeled, but you may wish to scout it out prior to the show. You won't have trouble finding it after that show as hundreds of fans will be surrounding the door.

About 20 minutes after the end of the show, cast members will slowly start to come out. Each one will draw loud cheers and tons of people will be holding up their phones for a coveted picture. Some cast members walk right out to a waiting car, while others will sign every autograph and take every picture requested.

INSIDER TIP!

There is no guarantee that the biggest stars will come out the stage door every night. You need to put some thought into increasing your chances. For instance, there are two full shows on Wednesday, meaning that the stars are tired late on Wednesday nights. The last time I was at the stage door on a Wednesday night, Lin-Manuel Miranda did not come out. He went straight home instead. If you put some thought and strategy into your best chance to catch a glimpse of the stars, hopefully you will get lucky!

The two most common requests at the stage door are for autographs and photos. People want their programs and other pictures and pieces of paper signed. You can take photos at any time, but you generally need to be in the front row to request a selfie with a cast member. Remember to be polite, safe, and respectful of other fans and the fact that the cast members are exhausted from performing on stage for nearly three hours!

Take what you can get and appreciate it. There is nothing like the experience of the *Hamilton* stage door!

INSIDER TIP!

If you leave the theater immediately after the show, there is definitely time to grab a slice of pizza at Patzeria across the street while you are waiting for the cast to come out the stage door. However, understand that doing so will put you further back in the crowd! Tough choice!

Section Three

ADDITIONAL INFORMATION

Chapter Twelve

CAST MEMBERS

*H*ere is a listing and a short description of each of the Original Broadway Cast Members of the musical *Hamilton*:

Alexander Hamilton is played by Lin-Manuel Miranda. The alternate is Javier Muñoz.

Lin-Manuel Miranda was born on January 16, 1980. He was the creator and star of the Broadway musical *In the Heights,* which opened on Broadway at the Richard Rodgers Theatre in March 2008. *In the Heights* won the 2008 Tony Award for Best Original Score and the 2009 Grammy Award for Best Musical Theater Album.

Lin-Manuel Miranda is also the creator and star of

the Broadway musical, *Hamilton*. This musical won the 2016 Grammy Award for Best Musical Theater Album.

Javier Muñoz grew up in Brooklyn, New York, and has starred in two hit Broadway musicals: *In the Heights* and *Hamilton*. In both productions, Javier Muñoz followed the creator and original star of the show, Lin-Manuel Miranda, in the lead role.

Javier Muñoz is the alternate for the role of Hamilton, usually performing on Sundays. He played the role of Alexander Hamilton the night President Barack Obama was at the show.

Aaron Burr is played by Leslie Odom, Jr.

Leslie Odom, Jr. was born on August 6, 1981. He played the role of Sam Strickland in the television series *Smash*. In addition to playing Aaron Burr in *Hamilton*, his theater credits include roles in *Dreamgirls, Leap of Faith, Venice, Witness Uganda,* and *Tick, Tick... Boom!* In addition to his role in *Smash,* he has also appeared in other television shows, including *The Big House, Threshold, Gilmore Girls, Vanished, Close To Home, Big Day, The Bill Engvall Show, Supreme Courtships, Grey's Anatomy, NCIS: Los Angeles, Zeke and Luther, Poe, House of Lies, Person of Interest, Law &*

Order: Special Victims Unit, The Good Wife, and *Gotham.*

Angelica Schuyler Church is played by Renée Elise Goldsberry.

Renée Elise Goldsberry was born on January 2, 1971. Her theater credits prior to starring in *Hamilton* include *The Lion King, Dreamgirls, Paper Moon, Abyssinia, Two Gentlemen of Verona, The Color Purple, The Baker's Wife, Rent, Good People, Love's Labor's Lost, As You Like It,* and *I'm Getting My Act Together and Taking it on the Road.* She has appeared in numerous television shows, including *Ally McBeal, Providence, Any Day Now, That 80's Show, Star Trek: Enterprise, One on One, One Life to Live, The Return of Jezebel James, Life on Mars, Royal Pains, White Collar, Running Wilde, The Good Wife, The Following, Save Me, Law & Order: Special Victims Unit, Masters of Sex,* and *Younger.*

Eliza Schuyler Hamilton is played by Phillipa Soo.

Phillipa Soo was born on May 31, 1990. Her previous acting experience includes playing the role of Natasha Rostova in *Natasha, Pierre & The Great Comet of 1812.* She has also appeared in the television show *Smash.*

Washington is played by Christopher n.

Christopher Jackson is from Illinois and has won both a Grammy Award and a Daytime Emmy Award. His previous theater work includes roles in *In the Heights, Bronx Bombers, After Midnight, The Lion King, Holler If Ya Hear Me*, and *Memphis.*

King George III was originally played by Jonathan Groff.

Jonathan Drew Groff was born on March 26, 1985. His theater credits include roles in *Fame, In My Life, Spring Awakening, Hair, Prayer for My Enemy, The Singing Forest, Deathtrap, The Submission*, and *Red*. In addition, he has appeared in numerous television shows including *One Life to Live, Pretty/Handsome, Glee, The Good Wife, Boss, Looking*, and *The Normal Heart.*

Maria Reynolds and Peggy Schuyler are played by Jasmine Cephas Jones.

Jasmine Cephas Jones was born on July 21, 1989. Prior to appearing in the musical *Hamilton,* she played the role of Kenisha in *The Loneliness of the Long Distance Runner*. Jasmine Cephas Jones has also appeared in numerous films and television shows, including *Blue Bloods, Fairfield, Unforgettable, Mistress America,* and *Titus.*

Thomas Jefferson and Marquis de Lafayette are played by Daveed Diggs.

Daveed Diggs was born on January 24, 1982. He is a member of the experimental hip-hop group, Clipping. Prior to starring in *Hamilton*, his theater credits include *Word Becomes Flesh*, *In the Red and Brown Water*, *Jesus Hopped the 'A' Train*, *The Tempest*, *Troilus and Cressida*, and *Mirrors in Every Corner.*

James Madison and Hercules Mulligan are played by Okieriete Onaodowan.

Okieriete Onaodowan grew up in New Jersey. His previous theater credits include *Rocky the Musical* on Broadway and the first national tour of *American Idiot.*

John Laurens and Philip Hamilton are played by Anthony Ramos.

Anthony Ramos was born on November 1, 1991. His previous theater credits include roles in *Grease*, *Damn Yankees*, *In the Heights*, and *21 Chump Street.*

Chapter Thirteen

MUSICAL NUMBERS
AND ALBUM SONGS

ere is a listing and short description of the musical numbers in *Hamilton* as they appear on the Original Cast Recording Album:

"Alexander Hamilton"
Full Company (except King George)

This is the opening number of the musical and not considered part of the narrative. The first and last musical numbers in the musical are outside of the narrative. Because of this, the cast wears different costumes during these songs. This song summarizes much of the plot and covers the early history of Alexander Hamilton prior to his arrival in North America.

"Aaron Burr, Sir"
Hamilton, Burr, Laurens, Lafayette, and Mulligan

This is the first song of the narrative, so it begins with the announcement that the year is 1776. This song introduces the two main characters, Alexander Hamilton and Aaron Burr, and their major characteristics. Alexander Hamilton is shown as driven and hoping others will recognize how smart he is. Aaron Burr is shown as changing his views, depending on his audience. The second part of the song introduces Hamilton's "crew" that will work with him throughout the Revolutionary War. In this part of the musical, Hamilton is trying to impress others with his intellect, so listen for intricate rhyming and rhythms!

"My Shot"
Hamilton, Burr, Laurens, Lafayette, Mulligan, and Company

This song took Lin-Manuel Miranda more than a year to write. Miranda needed that much time to come up with words that were nearly as brilliant as those Hamilton would have written! Filled with brilliant rap and rhyming, this is a huge crowd favorite.

"The Story of Tonight"
Hamilton, Laurens, Lafayette, Mulligan, and Company

Hamilton and his crew talk about their place in history and the moment that is upon them, a turning point in the history of the world. "Raise a glass to freedom" is first sung in this song, and the words will echo in sadness at the end of the musical.

"The Schuyler Sisters"
Angelica, Eliza, Peggy, Burr, and Company

Bring on the ladies! This song introduces the three Schuyler Sisters, daughters of the rich and influential Phillip Schuyler. Catching one of these three sisters would give Hamilton credibility and influence. The personality of the sisters is introduced in this number.

"Farmer Refuted"
Samuel Seabury and Hamilton

Samuel Seabury was a farmer who wanted the colonies to remain loyal to the British Monarchy. He states his case and then is shredded by Hamilton. Great interplay between the two characters … It is good on the album and unforgettable on stage!

"You'll be Back"
King George

This is our first introduction to King George, who sings three songs during the musical. Filled with irony and humor, his three songs are huge fan favorites.

"Right Hand Man"
Washington, Hamilton, Burr, and Company

This song introduces General George Washington and shows the start of the close relationship between Washington and Hamilton. It also introduces the first sign of Hamilton's dissatisfaction with being an aide to General Washington, instead of leading his own troops. This conflict will run throughout the first act. The close relationship between Hamilton and Washington runs throughout the full musical and is key to much of Hamilton's success. Among the events covered in this song is the brave (or crazy) act of Hamilton stealing British cannons.

"A Winter's Ball"
Burr, Hamilton, and Laurens

Hamilton, Burr, and Laurens show up at a ball in the city to meet some ladies. Hamilton impresses. Burr does not. The next two songs show the introduction to his future wife, Eliza, through their marriage from two different points of view. The first song narrates the events from Eliza's point of view, followed by a song reflecting the same events from the perspective of her sister, Angelica.

"Helpless"
Eliza, Hamilton, and Company

Hamilton meets Angelica Schuyler at a ball in 1780. Angelica takes him across the room and introduces him to her sister, Eliza Schuyler. Eliza falls in love, and after a courtship, they marry.

"Satisfied"
Angelica, Hamilton, and Company

This song covers the same events from Angelica's point of view. It begins at the wedding and then "rewinds" back to the point of introduction. Angelica clearly is attracted to Hamilton but lets her sister have him out of kindness and her obligation to marry a financial provider. Angelica and Alexander Hamilton would remain very close throughout the rest of their lives. Angelica was present when Hamilton died, and they are both buried at Trinity Church in New York.

"The Story of Tonight" (Reprise)
Hamilton, Burr, Laurens, Lafayette, and Mulligan

Hamilton and his crew together after the wedding. A fun play on the words "Raise a glass to freedom" and fun interplay between characters that love each other … until Aaron Burr shows up.

"Wait for It"
Burr and Company

This song sums up Aaron Burr's philosophy on life: Wait for it and good things will come to you. Don't stick your neck out, and it can never get cut off. This is in sharp contrast to Hamilton's philosophy. This song also introduces us to Aaron Burr's love, Theodosia, who is married to a British loyalist.

"Stay Alive"
Hamilton, Washington, Charles Lee, Laurens, and Company

The war is not going well, and in this song, Hamilton and Washington adjust the strategy they are using to battle the British.

"Ten Duel Commandments"
Laurens, Hamilton, Lee, Burr, and Company

The first of three duels in the musical is recounted here. This dues is between Charles Lee (who was being critical of Washington) and John Laurens. Hamilton accompanies Laurens as his "second," while Aaron Burr accompanies Charles Lee. The song explains the rules and traditions of dueling.

"Meet Me Inside"
Washington, Hamilton, and Company

Washington is not happy that Hamilton was at the duel, and he and Hamilton argue. By the end of this song, Hamilton resigns his position as Washington's aide. This event happened in January of 1881.

"That Would be Enough"
Eliza and Hamilton

Back home with his wife, Eliza, Alexander Hamilton learns that Eliza is pregnant. This song expresses the wish that just living a simple life with no advancement would be enough for Hamilton.

"Guns and Ships"
Burr, Lafayette and Washington

This song features the amazing rap artistry of Lafayette, and true fans will learn the song and try to sing it at Lafayette's pace! The song is about the French siding with the colonies and providing guns and ships at Lafayette's request. It also covers Hamilton returning to the war to lead troops.

"History Has Its Eyes on You"
Washington and Company

A short song with Washington talking to Hamilton about leading troops into battle. Like a father talking to his son, Washington is telling Hamilton that this is the moment the whole world is watching. The words "Who lives, who dies, who tells your story?" are introduced in this song.

"Yorktown (The World Turned Upside Down)"
Hamilton, Lafayette, Laurens, Mulligan, and Company

The last battle of the Revolutionary War was the battle of Yorktown in 1781. Hamilton and Lafayette are instrumental in the victory, as is their friend, Hercules Mulligan. George Washington accepts the surrender of the British, and the celebration begins as the colonies realize they have won.

"What Comes Next?"
King George

The second song by King George has him in disbelief that this small group of colonies has defeated his global superpower.

"Dear Theodosia"
Burr and Hamilton

One of the most beautiful songs in the musical, Burr and Hamilton are alone on stage, sitting in chairs and singing about their children. Burr's daughter, Theodosia, is named after her mother. Hamilton's son, Philip, is named after his grandfather. It is a beautiful recognition that the birth of a nation will coincide with these children growing up.

"Non-Stop"
Hamilton, Burr, Eliza, Angelica, Washington, and Company

The final song of the first act covers the major events right after the war. Hamilton and Burr are co-counsel in the first murder trial in the new nation. Hamilton is driven and instrumental in defending and interpreting the new Constitution. Burr as usual refuses to take sides. The song show the unbelievable amount of writing that Hamilton was capable of and his non-stop efforts toward the success of the new nation. A great and rousing finish to the first act.

"What'd I Miss"
Burr, Jefferson, Madison, and Company

The second act of the musical does not include Lafayette, so the actor playing that character switches and now plays Thomas Jefferson. Jefferson spent the war in France. In this song, he returns and sets up the events of the second act.

"Cabinet Battle #1"
Washington, Jefferson, Hamilton, and Madison

Hamilton and Jefferson would battle countless times after the war as the new government was established. This first epic rap battle is about whether or not the new national government should assume the debts of the states. As was usually the case, Jefferson and James Madison, both from Virginia, would be Hamilton's biggest opponents.

"Take a Break"
Eliza, Philip, Hamilton, and Angelica

Hamilton goes home to work but needs to return to New York to get his banking plan through Congress. Angelica and Eliza want him to stay in the country for the summer, but Hamilton returns to New York. The beginning of this song introduces Hamilton's son, Philip, at the age of nine.

"Say No to This"
Hamilton, Maria Reynolds, James Reynolds, and Company

While working in New York away from his wife, Hamilton has an affair with Maria Reynolds. Her husband, James Reynolds, blackmails Hamilton.

"The Room Where It Happens"
Burr, Hamilton, Jefferson, Madison, and Company

Hamilton meets with Jefferson and Madison to hammer out a compromise on Hamilton's banking plan. In the end, the nation's capitol is moved to Virginia, and Hamilton gets the votes for his banking plan. The subplot of this song is that Aaron Burr would give anything to be "in the room where it happens," but he is not in a position of power.

"Schuyler Defeated"
Philip, Eliza, Hamilton, and Burr

Aaron Burr runs in an election against Philip Schuyler and defeats him. This song once again shows Burr shifting positions to gain political advantage.

"Cabinet Battle #2"
Washington, Jefferson, Hamilton, and Madison

The second cabinet rap battle is over the issue of helping the French in their revolution. Once again, Hamilton is up against Jefferson and Madison. Jefferson wants to join the French as was promised, while Hamilton feels we should not. Hamilton wins this battle, leaving Jefferson so mad he will eventually resign in order to run for president.

"Washington on Your Side"
Burr, Jefferson, and Madison

Jefferson makes the decision that he needs to resign and run for the presidency. This is the start of political parties in the United States. Jefferson decides to dig up dirt on Hamilton.

"One Last Time"
Washington, Hamilton, and Company

Washington announces that he is not running for a third term as president. He has Hamilton write his final speech, one of the most influential speeches ever in American politics.

"I Know Him"
King George

The final song by King George finds him confused that a national leader can just quit. That would never happen in a monarchy. King George remembers John Adams but is not impressed. This is your last chance to show your love to one of the show's best-drawn characters.

"The Adams Administration"
Burr, Hamilton, and Company

Hamilton is fired from the John Adams administration. Jefferson finishes second in the election and, therefore, is Vice President.

"We Know"
Burr, Hamilton, Jefferson, and Madison

Hamilton writes articles against the administration, so Jefferson and Madison accuse Hamilton of speculation. Hamilton tells them he was not stealing money—he was being blackmailed by the husband after having an affair with the man's wife.

"Hurricane"
Hamilton and Company

Hamilton's story begins with a hurricane on the Caribbean Island where he lived. He now finds himself in another hurricane, this one political. Hamilton is afraid his political enemies will tell people about his affair with Maria Reynolds, so he decides to write about it himself.

"The Reynolds Pamphlet"
Full Company

Hamilton publishes the account of his affair with Maria Reynolds. This ends his political career. Jefferson and Madison celebrate.

"Burn"
Eliza

Eliza is crushed by the news of the affair and the fact that Hamilton would make it public. A heart-crushing song.

"Blow Us All Away"
Philip, George Eacker, Hamilton, and Company

George Eacker is being critical of Alexander Hamilton, so Philip Hamilton challenges him to a duel. Alexander gives his son some advice and send him off. Philip is shot by Eacker.

"Stay Alive" (Reprise)
Philip, Hamilton, Eliza, Doctor

Philip Hamilton dies in the arms of his mother after the duel.

"It's Quiet Uptown"
Angelica, Hamilton, Eliza, and Company

Alexander and Eliza Hamilton mourn the death of their son and their happy marriage.

"The Election of 1800"
Jefferson, Madison, Burr, Hamilton, and Company

Jefferson and Burr run against each other for the presidency in 1800. The election is a tie in the Electoral College, and Hamilton is asked who he supports. Hamilton sides with Jefferson because Jefferson has strong views and Burr has none. Even though Jefferson and Hamilton have battled over the years, Hamilton respects someone with strong convictions.

"Your Obedient Servant"
Burr, Hamilton

Burr realizes that Hamilton has been an obstacle to his success throughout his life and challenges him to a duel.

"Best of Wives and Best of Women"
Eliza, Hamilton

A short song with Hamilton writing his final letter to his wife before the duel. Columbia University in New York has the original letter on their campus. Lin-Manuel Miranda has tweeted a picture of the letter. The words "Best of Wives and Best of Women" are his haunting final words to Eliza.

"The World was Wide Enough"
Burr, Hamilton, and Company

Hamilton and Burr duel, and Hamilton is shot and killed. In part of this song, Aaron Burr recognizes that the world was large enough for both of them to succeed. The highlight of the song is Hamilton's final barrage of words as he watches the fatal bullet approach him in slow motion.

"Who Lives, Who Dies, Who Tells Your Story"
Eliza, and Full Company

The final song allows other characters to speak about Hamilton. Jefferson and Madison are complementary. Eliza lived for 50 years after

Hamilton died and spends much of that time preserving his legacy.

Chapter Fourteen

LIST OF CHARACTERS

*H*ere is a listing and short description of each of the characters in the musical *Hamilton*.

Alexander Hamilton

If you don't know who Alexander Hamilton is by this point ... you should read Chapter 3!

Aaron Burr

First a friend and then a rival of Hamilton's, the stories of Aaron Burr story and Hamilton will forever be intertwined. Aaron Burr was an officer in the Revolutionary War, a member of the New York State Assembly, and a U.S. Senator. He was also Vice President of the United States under Thomas

Jefferson. Aaron Burr killed Alexander Hamilton in a duel, and although all charges against him were dropped, the event ended his political career.

George Washington

A key mentor in the life of Hamilton, Washington's friendship and support over the years increased Hamilton's stature and influence. George Washington was the Commander-in-Chief of the Continental Army during the Revolutionary War. He presided over the convention that drafted the current U.S. Constitution. He was the first President of the United States.

Angelica Schuyler Church

Angelica Schuyler was the oldest daughter of Philip Schuyler, a General in the Continental Army during the Revolutionary War. She was the wife of John Barker Church and the sister of Alexander Hamilton's wife, Elizabeth Schuyler.

Elizabeth Schuyler Hamilton

Elizabeth Schuyler Hamilton, often called "Eliza," was the daughter of Philip Schuyler, a General in the Continental Army during the Revolutionary War, and the wife of Alexander Hamilton. She lived for 50 years after Alexander Hamilton's death. During that time, she preserved his writings and his legacy and co-founded the first orphanage in New York City.

King George III

King George III was the King of Great Britain from January, 1801 until his death in January, 1820. His reign was longer than any other British monarch before him, and it was filled with military conflicts throughout the world. He was the monarch when Great Britain was defeated by the American colonies in the Revolutionary War.

Maria Reynolds

In 1791, Maria Reynolds began a two-year affair with Alexander Hamilton. She was 23 years old at the time. Maria's husband, James Reynolds, was aware of the affair and used it to blackmail money from Hamilton. The affair became public when Hamilton published the Reynolds Pamphlet, giving the details of the affair and the blackmail that followed.

Peggy Schuyler

Peggy Schuyler was the oldest daughter of Philip Schuyler, a General in the Continental Army during the Revolutionary War. She was the sister of Alexander Hamilton's wife, Elizabeth Schuyler.

Thomas Jefferson

Thomas Jefferson was born in Virginia in 1743. During the Revolutionary War, he became the United States Minister to France. After the war, he was the nation's first Secretary of State. Jefferson and James Madison started the Democratic-Republican Party to oppose the Federalist Party. He was elected the third President of the United States.

Marquis de Lafayette

Marquis de Lafayette was a French military officer who fought for the United States in the Revolutionary War. He was a close friend of George Washington, Alexander Hamilton, and Thomas Jefferson. Lafayette was also a key figure in the French Revolution of 1789.

James Madison

James Madison was a member of the Continental Congress prior to the Constitutional Convention. After the Convention, he was one of the leaders in the movement to ratify the Constitution. He wrote The Federalist Papers, along with Alexander Hamilton and John Jay. Madison started the Democratic-Republican Party with Thomas Jefferson. He served as Secretary of State under

President Jefferson, and after that became the fourth President of the United States.

Hercules Mulligan

Hercules Mulligan was born in Ireland and came to the United States in 1746. He lived with Alexander Hamilton in New York when they both attended King's College. During the Revolutionary War, Mulligan began spying on the British Government, smuggling key information to the colonial forces.

John Laurens

John Laurens was born in South Carolina in 1754. During the Revolutionary War, he helped recruit slaves to fight against the British. He was killed in the Battle of the Combahee River in August, 1782.

Philip Hamilton

Philip Hamilton was the oldest son of Alexander Hamilton. He graduated from King's College, just like his father. Philip was killed at the age of 19 in a duel with George Eacker. He died in the home of Angelica Schuyler with both of his parents at his side.

Chapter Fifteen

WEBSITES TO VISIT

There are a number of websites that will give you more information about Alexander Hamilton and the show. Here are a few that I recommend.

Hamilton - Official Broadway Site

www.hamiltonbroadway.com

This is the official site of the musical and a great source of information about the musical. A complete show calendar with show times and cast updates can be found here. You can also enter the daily ticket lottery here and watch the Ham4Ham videos.

Hamilton - Broadway Tickets | Broadway | Broadway...

www.broadway.com/shows/hamilton-broadway

This is a great site for all shows on Broadway. When scheduling your trip to New York, this is a great site to choose other shows and get great information about all of Broadway!

Hamilton on Wikipedia

en.wikipedia.org/wiki/Hamilton_(musical)

Wikipedia is a great place to get a summary of information about the show, the cast, and the team behind the musical. Follow each link to learn more about the characters, each cast member, and the history of the musical!

Stubhub Tickets

www.Stubhub.com

Tickets to *Hamilton* are difficult to get through the box office and official website, but there are many tickets available through StubHub. Check out a variety of dates to get the lowest prices, and be sure to print your tickets before you arrive at the theater … they will not print them for you!

Broadway in Chicago - Official Site

broadwayinchicago.com

The second location to host a version of *Hamilton* will be Chicago! Get the latest news on tickets, dates, and show times at the official Broadway in Chicago website!

Restaurant Row

http://www.restaurantrownyc.com/

Dozens of restaurants within two blocks of the Richard Rodgers Theatre … you are sure to find one you like!

Chapter Sixteen

TWITTER ACCOUNTS TO FOLLOW

Many of the original cast members are on Twitter; following them will give you a great deal of information about what they are doing and when they are going to be in the show. (It will also often give you a clue about when they are not going to be in the show!)

Here is a list of Twitter accounts for some of the original cast members. As new cast members are added to the show, you can often find their Twitter accounts by reading other cast members' tweets.

The official Twitter feed of Hamilton the Musical is @HamiltonMusical

Lin-Manuel Miranda - @Lin_Manuel

Javier Muñoz - @JMunozActor

Leslie Odom, Jr. - @leslieodomjr

Renée Elise Goldsberry - @reneeelisegolds

Phillipa Soo - @Phillipasoo

Christopher Jackson - @ChrisisSingin

Daveed Diggs - @DaveedDiggs

Okieriete Onaodowan

Anthony Ramos - @Anthony_Ramos1

Chapter Seventeen

ADDITIONAL READING

Hamilton: The Revolution
Published: April 12, 2016
by Lin-Manuel Miranda and Jeremy McCarter

Hamilton - Vocal Selections
Published: April 1, 2016
by Lin-Manuel Miranda

Alexander Hamilton
Published: March 29, 2005
by Ron Chernow

Hamilton: The History Behind the Revolutionary Musical
Published: March 1, 2016
by Kristine Dawson

The Hamilton (musical) Handbook - Everything You Need to Know about Hamilton (musical)
Published: April 13, 2016
by Madison Huber

Alexander Hamilton: The Outsider
Published: January 6, 2011
by Jean Fritz

The Complete Works of Alexander Hamilton
Published: September 16, 2011
by Alexander Hamilton and Henry Cabot Lodge

Chapter Eighteen

HAMILTON GEAR AND SOUVENIRS

*D*on't let one of the greatest experiences of your life go by without getting a souvenir! When it comes to impressive gear and mementos, *Hamilton* doesn't disappoint. Fans have plenty to choose from; there's a large assortment of *Hamilton* apparel, including t-shirts for guys and gals, hoodies, and caps. You'll also find plenty of gift and practical items that will remind you of the musical for years to come.

To get your official *Hamilton* apparel, visit:

www.broadwaymerchandiseshop.com/stores/
hamilton/apparel

(T-shirts, Hoodies, Ball Caps, Ski Caps)

There are also find incredible *Hamilton* souvenirs to keep or share. Don't fret—there's something for everyone, and almost of all of it proudly displays the cool one-of-a-kind *Hamilton* star logo! Find just what you're looking for at:

www.broadwaymerchandiseshop.com/stores/ hamilton/souvenirs

(Notebooks, cards, pins, magnets, mugs, totes, water bottles, books, etc.)

INSIDER TIP!

While there's plenty to choose from, *Hamilton* merchandise and apparel are popular and do sell out. Don't wait until you see the show to get your *Hamilton* merchandise! Get it before you see the show—you won't be sorry!

Made in the USA
San Bernardino, CA
11 December 2016